Drive and Survive

WINTER DRIVING IN CANADA

What Every Driver Needs to Know
When Conditions Turn Dangerous

A Practical Safety Guide

Printed in Canada

ABOUT DRIVE & SURVIVE

Drive & Survive was created to address a simple reality: Canadian winter driving is often underestimated. Experience alone does not prevent accidents—preparation, judgment, and respect for conditions do.

The Drive & Survive approach focuses on practical, real-world decision-making rather than fear or bravado. The goal is not to encourage drivers to push through dangerous conditions, but to help them recognize risk early, prepare properly, and make safer choices for themselves, their passengers, and their communities.

This guide reflects that philosophy, bringing together clear guidance, common-sense preparation, and real-world winter driving awareness designed specifically for Canadian roads and winter conditions.

TABLE OF CONTENTS

Introduction

About the Author

Wade Chapman is a professional Class 1 driver and instructor with more than four decades of experience operating commercial vehicles across North America. Over the course of his career, he has driven more than three million miles in some of the most demanding and unforgiving conditions on the continent.

Wade's experience includes repeated winter travel on British Columbia's Coquihalla Highway—often referred to as the *"Highway Through Hell"*—as well as fuel truck operations throughout the Kootenays during extreme winter conditions. For the past twenty-six years, his work has focused primarily on the mountainous regions of British Columbia and western Washington, where winter driving requires constant vigilance, restraint, and respect for rapidly changing conditions.

In addition to his driving career, Wade has served as a Class 1 instructor in both Ontario and British Columbia, training drivers in vehicle control, winter operations, and professional decision-making. His background includes experience as a skid school trainer, where drivers learn how vehicles behave at the limits of traction and how to respond when control is lost.

Throughout his career, Wade has operated a wide range of commercial equipment, including tanker trucks, lowbeds, trailers, and B-trains. His approach to winter driving instruction is grounded in real-world experience rather than theory, emphasizing preparation, awareness, and the understanding that no amount of confidence or experience can override road conditions.

This guide reflects a lifetime of professional driving, instruction, and observation. It is written for everyday drivers with the same philosophy Wade has applied throughout his career: winter driving is not about skill alone—it is about judgment, patience, and respect for the road.

Regardless of experience level, Wade maintains that winter driving demands humility, because when conditions turn dangerous, experience does not change the laws of physics.

Chapter 1

Before You Leave: Planning Your Winter Trip

Winter driving in Canada is less about confidence behind the wheel and more about the decisions made before the engine starts. Roads that appear manageable at departure can quickly become dangerous due to snow, ice, wind, temperature changes, or reduced visibility. Regardless of experience, winter conditions demand preparation, awareness, and a willingness to adjust plans when conditions change.

One of the most common winter driving mistakes is underestimating how quickly conditions can deteriorate. A trip that begins on clear pavement can turn into a hazardous drive within minutes, especially in rural areas, mountain passes, or during rapidly moving weather systems. Planning ahead allows drivers to identify risks early and avoid unnecessary exposure to dangerous conditions.

Checking the Weather Forecast

Weather forecasts should always be reviewed before any winter trip, even short ones. Focus on more than just temperature or snowfall totals. Pay close attention to wind, freezing rain warnings, blowing snow advisories, and rapid temperature drops that can cause black ice.
Winter weather systems can vary significantly by region. Conditions may be clear in one area while dangerous just a short distance away. When travelling longer distances, check forecasts for your departure point, destination, and any major areas along your route.

If weather warnings or advisories are in effect, consider delaying travel until conditions improve. No appointment or schedule is worth risking personal safety.

Checking Road Conditions and Reports

Before travelling, review official road condition reports for your route. Provincial highway reporting systems provide valuable information about:

- Road surface conditions
- Visibility concerns
- Accidents or closures
- Maintenance activity such as plowing or sanding

Road conditions can change quickly, particularly overnight or during storms. A road reported as "open" does not mean it is safe to travel. "Open" simply means it has not been officially closed. Drivers must still assess whether conditions are appropriate for their vehicle, experience level, and travel purpose.

Using Highway Webcams

Highway webcams offer real-time visibility into road and weather conditions that written reports may not fully capture. Webcams can reveal:

- Actual visibility levels
- Snow accumulation
- Traffic flow
- Wind effects and drifting snow

Checking webcams along your route provides a realistic picture of what you are about to encounter. If visibility appears poor or conditions look worse than expected, it may be safer to delay or cancel travel.

Planning for Time and Daylight

Winter travel often takes longer than expected. Snow-covered roads, reduced speed, traffic delays, and weather-related incidents can significantly increase travel time.

Plan trips during daylight whenever possible. Visibility is reduced at night in winter conditions, and hazards such as ice, snowdrifts, wildlife, and pedestrians are more difficult to see. If travel after dark is unavoidable, allow extra time and reduce speed accordingly.

Letting Someone Know Your Plans

For longer trips or travel through rural or remote areas, always let someone know your route and expected arrival time. Share:

- Departure time
- Planned route
- Destination
- Estimated arrival time

If plans change, update your contact when possible. This simple step can be critical if assistance is needed and communication becomes limited.

Deciding When Not to Go

One of the most important winter driving skills is knowing when not to drive. Choosing to delay or cancel a trip is not a failure — it is responsible decision-making.

Consider postponing travel if:

- Weather warnings are active
- Visibility is poor
- Roads are icy or snow-covered
- You feel fatigued, unwell, or unprepared
- Your vehicle is not fully winter-ready

Regardless of experience, winter conditions are the great equalizer. Every driver is subject to the same laws of physics when traction is reduced.

Final Thought Before You Leave

Winter driving safety begins long before the wheels turn. Taking time to assess weather, road conditions, visibility, and personal readiness can prevent many winter emergencies before they occur.
The safest winter trip is often the one that waits for better conditions.

Chapter 2

Preparing Your Vehicle for Winter

Winter driving safety depends as much on the condition of your vehicle as it does on driver skill. In cold temperatures, even well-maintained vehicles can behave differently. Batteries weaken, tires lose flexibility, fluids thicken, and visibility becomes more difficult to maintain. Preparing your vehicle before winter travel is essential for reducing risk and preventing breakdowns.

A vehicle that performs well in summer conditions may not be adequately prepared for snow, ice, and extreme cold. Regular seasonal checks and proper winter equipment can make a critical difference when conditions deteriorate.

Tires and Traction

Tires are the single most important safety feature on your vehicle during winter driving. Winter-rated tires are designed to remain flexible in cold temperatures and provide improved traction on snow and ice.

All-season tires may be acceptable in mild conditions but often lose effectiveness as temperatures drop. If you regularly drive in snow, ice, or sub-zero temperatures, dedicated winter tires are strongly recommended.

Check tire pressure regularly during winter. Cold temperatures cause air pressure to drop, and under-inflated tires reduce traction and handling. Ensure tire tread depth is sufficient to channel snow and slush away from the tire surface.

Battery Readiness

Cold temperatures significantly reduce battery performance. A battery that functions adequately in warmer months may fail without warning in winter.

Have your battery tested before winter, especially if it is more than a few years old. Watch for slow engine cranking, dim lights, or electrical issues, which may indicate a weakening battery.

Carry jumper cables or a portable battery booster in your vehicle at all times. A dead battery is one of the most common winter roadside issues and can often be resolved quickly if you are prepared.

Engine Fluids and Winter Ratings

Ensure all vehicle fluids are appropriate for winter temperatures. This includes:

- Engine oil rated for cold weather operation
- Coolant with proper antifreeze protection
- Transmission and brake fluids in good condition

Windshield washer fluid must be rated for freezing temperatures. Summer washer fluid can freeze, crack reservoirs, and leave you without visibility when you need it most.

Visibility and Lighting

Visibility is one of the greatest challenges during winter driving. Snow, ice, salt spray, and low light conditions can quickly reduce a driver's ability to see and be seen.

Always clear all snow and ice from your vehicle before driving. This includes:

- Windshield
- Side and rear windows
- Mirrors
- Headlights and taillights
- Roof and hood

Partial clearing is dangerous and often illegal. Ice or snow sliding from a vehicle can obscure your view or strike other vehicles and pedestrians.

Keep these areas clear of snow

Windshield Wipers and Ice Removal

Ensure windshield wipers are in good condition and rated for winter use. Worn or frozen wipers can smear slush and ice, reducing visibility. Carry a sturdy ice scraper or window scraping tool. Improvised tools or credit cards are ineffective and may damage glass. Take time to fully clear windows and mirrors before driving.

Headlights — More Than Daytime Running Lights

In winter conditions, daytime running lights are not sufficient. Many vehicles with daytime running lights do not activate rear lights, making the vehicle difficult to see from behind in snow, fog, or reduced visibility.

Always turn on your full headlights when driving in winter conditions, even during daylight hours. Full headlights ensure both front and rear lights are illuminated, improving visibility for other drivers.

A simple rule:
If your windshield wipers are on, your headlights should be on.

DAYTIME RUNNING LIGHTS   **FULL HEADLIGHTS**

Emergency Equipment and Preparedness

Beyond routine vehicle maintenance, winter preparedness includes carrying essential emergency equipment. A basic winter emergency kit should include:

- Jumper cables or a battery booster
- Ice scraper and snow brush
- Flashlight and spare batteries
- Reflective warning triangles or flares
- Warm blankets or extra clothing

Preparation does not eliminate winter risk, but it significantly improves your ability to respond safely when something goes wrong.

Final Vehicle Preparation Check

Before any winter trip, take a few minutes to assess your vehicle's readiness. Confirm that tires, battery, lights, fluids, and emergency supplies are in good condition.

Winter driving begins with preparation. A few preventative steps can reduce stress, prevent breakdowns, and improve safety for you and others on the road.

Chapter 3

Winter Emergency Kit Essentials

Even the best planning and vehicle preparation cannot eliminate all winter driving risks. Road closures, sudden storms, mechanical failures, and traffic incidents can leave drivers stranded with little warning. A properly stocked winter emergency kit can make a critical difference in comfort, safety, and survival while waiting for assistance.

Many winter emergencies do not involve dramatic accidents. More often, drivers become delayed or disabled due to weather, dead batteries, or road conditions. Being prepared allows you to stay safe and calm while help arrives.

Why an Emergency Kit Matters

Winter conditions can slow or prevent emergency response. Roadside assistance, tow trucks, and emergency services may be delayed during storms or widespread incidents. In rural or remote areas, response times can be significantly longer.

An emergency kit provides the basic resources needed to remain warm, visible, and safe while waiting. It also allows you to assist yourself or others in minor situations without relying immediately on outside help.

Warmth and Personal Safety

Maintaining body heat is the top priority if you become stranded in winter. Even inside a vehicle, temperatures can drop quickly.

Include items such as:

- Warm blankets or sleeping bags
- Extra winter clothing, including hats, gloves, and socks
- Chemical hand or body warmers
- An emergency shelter or tarp (optional but recommended)

These items help prevent hypothermia and maintain comfort during extended waits.

Visibility and Signaling

If your vehicle is disabled, it must be visible to other drivers and emergency responders.

Essential visibility items include:

- Reflective warning triangles or roadside flares
- A flashlight with spare batteries
- A whistle or signaling device

Using hazard lights and reflective equipment reduces the risk of secondary collisions and helps responders locate you more quickly.

Food and Hydration

Stranded drivers may be delayed for hours. Food and water help maintain energy, focus, and warmth.

Include:
- Non-perishable, high-energy food
- Bottled water (replace if frozen or damaged)
- A thermos with a warm beverage for longer trips

Avoid foods that require cooking or special preparation.

First Aid and Health Supplies

A basic first aid kit should be part of every winter emergency kit. Include:

- Bandages and basic wound care supplies
- Personal medications as appropriate
- Copies of important medical information

If you rely on medical devices or treatments, ensure you have backup supplies when travelling in winter conditions.

Battery and Breakdown Essentials

Cold temperatures are hard on vehicle batteries. A dead battery is one of the most common winter breakdowns.

Always carry:

- Jumper cables in good condition or a charged portable battery booster
- Gloves suitable for handling cables in cold weather
- Basic knowledge of safe boosting procedures

Being able to boost your own vehicle or accept help safely can prevent extended delays.

Tools and Traction Aids

Basic tools can help resolve minor winter issues or improve traction.

Consider including:

- A small shovel
- Traction aids such as sand, gravel, or traction mats
- A multi-tool or basic tool kit

These items may help you free a stuck vehicle or make small adjustments safely.

Communications and Navigation

Maintaining communication is critical during winter travel. Include:

- A phone charging cable compatible with your vehicle
- A backup battery pack
- A paper map in case GPS or cellular service fails

Cold temperatures can reduce battery life, so keep devices warm when possible.

Pets Travelling With You

If you travel with pets, your emergency kit must include their needs. Include:

- A pet carrier or proper restraint
- A blanket or insulation for warmth
- Extra pet food and water
- A copy of pet emergency contact information

In the event of an accident, emergency responders may not know a pet is present unless it is clearly documented.

Emergency Kit Checklist

Your winter emergency kit should be checked at the start of each season and before long trips. Replace expired, damaged, or missing items, and adjust supplies based on travel distance, weather conditions, and passengers.

Preparation does not eliminate winter risk—but it significantly improves outcomes when something goes wrong.

Chapter 4

Driving Safely in Winter Conditions

Winter driving requires a different approach than driving in dry, summer conditions. Reduced traction, limited visibility, and unpredictable surfaces demand slower speeds, smoother inputs, and greater awareness of surrounding hazards. Even small mistakes can have serious consequences when roads are icy or snow-covered.

Safe winter driving is not about confidence or speed. It is about maintaining control, allowing space for error, and recognizing when conditions exceed safe limits.

Speed and Following Distance

Speed is the most critical factor in winter driving safety. Driving too fast for conditions reduces your ability to stop, steer, and respond to unexpected hazards.

Reduce speed well below posted limits when roads are snow-covered or icy. Posted speed limits are designed for ideal conditions, not winter weather.

Increase following distance significantly. In winter conditions, you may need three to four times the normal distance to stop safely. This extra space provides time to react if the vehicle ahead slows suddenly or loses control.

SUMMER CONDITIONS

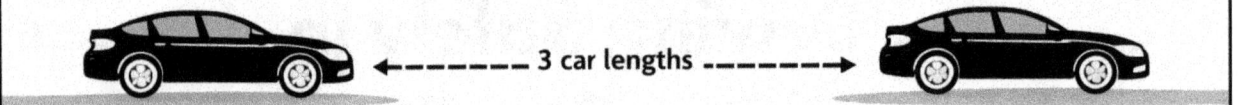

3 car lengths

WINTER CONDITIONS

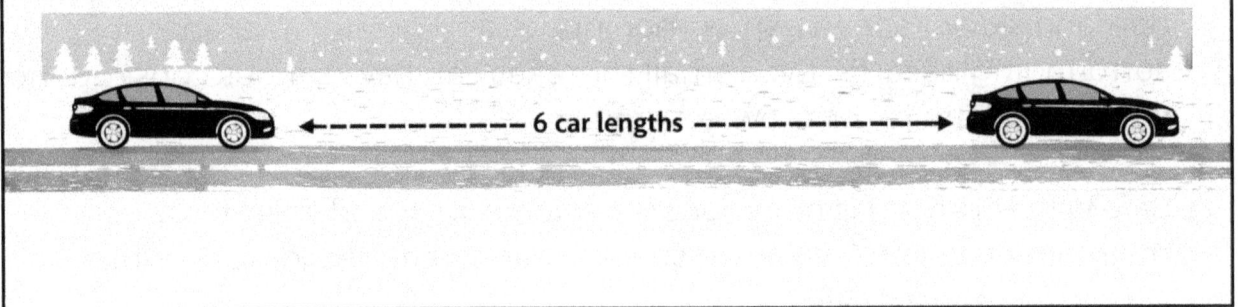

6 car lengths

Please note: image is not to scale and is only to get the idea across

Braking on Snow and Ice

Sudden or aggressive braking can cause wheels to lock and result in loss of control. Apply brakes smoothly and gradually whenever possible.

If your vehicle is equipped with anti-lock braking (ABS), press the brake pedal firmly and allow the system to work. You may feel vibration or hear noise—this is normal. Do not pump the brakes.

If traction is extremely limited, gently easing off the brake can sometimes help regain control.

Steering and Vehicle Control

Steering inputs should be smooth and deliberate. Sharp or sudden steering movements can cause a vehicle to slide.
If your vehicle begins to skid:

- Remain calm
- Ease off the accelerator
- Steer gently in the direction you want the front of the vehicle to go
- Avoid over-correcting

Regaining control takes patience and restraint.

Cornering and Turning at Intersections

Intersections are high-risk areas in winter due to braking, turning, and cross traffic.

Approach corners slowly and begin braking well before the turn. Avoid braking hard while turning, as this can cause loss of traction.

When turning at intersections, do not cut corners tightly. Make wider turns to allow space for recovery if the vehicle begins to slide. Wide turns also reduce the risk of striking parked vehicles or pedestrians.

Stopping at Traffic Lights and Hills

Stopping on icy surfaces requires planning. Begin slowing early and use gentle braking. If you notice vehicles sliding or struggling ahead, increase following distance further.

On hills, maintain steady momentum and avoid stopping if possible. If you encounter a hill where vehicles are sliding backward or unable to climb, do not proceed. Turn around safely or wait until conditions improve.

Parking Lots and Pedestrian Areas

Parking lots can be deceptively dangerous in winter. Ice, packed snow, and limited visibility create hazards even at low speeds.

Slow down significantly and watch carefully for pedestrians, pets, and children. Vehicles may slide unexpectedly around corners, and people walking may be difficult to see.

Winter driving safety applies everywhere—not just highways.

Visibility and Awareness

Snowfall, blowing snow, fog, and darkness reduce visibility quickly. Keep headlights on at all times in winter conditions, not just daytime running lights.

Watch for brake lights ahead and be alert to sudden stops. If visibility drops significantly, reduce speed immediately or consider pulling over in a safe location until conditions improve.

Knowing When to Stop Driving

There are times when the safest decision is to stop driving altogether. Whiteout conditions, freezing rain, or severe icing can make travel unsafe regardless of skill or equipment.

If you feel uncertain or overwhelmed, find a safe place to pull over and wait. Choosing to stop is not a failure—it is responsible winter driving.

Final Reminder

Winter driving safety depends on patience, preparation, and respect for conditions. Slowing down, allowing space, and avoiding unnecessary risks can prevent many winter collisions.

Every winter drive is different. Adjust accordingly.

Chapter 5

Towns, Cities and Communities

Winter driving is not limited to highways and long-distance travel. In towns and cities, winter conditions create a different set of risks that are often underestimated. Lower speeds do not eliminate danger when roads are icy, visibility is reduced, and pedestrians are present.

Urban and residential winter driving requires heightened awareness, patience, and respect for shared spaces.

Urban Winter Driving Hazards

City driving introduces frequent stops, intersections, crosswalks, and tight turns. Snowbanks can reduce sight-lines, hide curbs, and narrow lanes. Ice buildup near intersections and bus stops increases the risk of sliding during braking or turning.

Traffic congestion can also create unpredictable conditions, with sudden stops and lane changes. Winter driving in cities demands constant scanning and anticipation.

Intersections and Crosswalks

Intersections are among the most dangerous locations in winter. Vehicles may slide through stop signs or traffic lights, and pedestrians may struggle to maintain footing while crossing.

Approach intersections slowly and be prepared for vehicles or pedestrians behaving unpredictably. Begin braking earlier than usual and allow extra time to come to a complete stop.

Always scan sidewalks and crosswalks carefully. Snowbanks and parked vehicles can obstruct your view of pedestrians stepping into the roadway.

Turning Safely in Towns and Cities

When turning in winter conditions, avoid cutting corners tightly. Make wide, controlled turns to allow room for correction if the vehicle begins to slide.

Wide turns also reduce the risk of striking parked vehicles, curbs, cyclists, or pedestrians who may be walking close to the roadway due to snow-covered sidewalks.

Signal early and clearly, and be prepared to adjust if traction is limited.

Parking Lots and Shared Spaces

Parking lots require special caution in winter. Ice is often compacted and polished by vehicle traffic, making traction unpredictable.

Slow down significantly when entering or exiting parking lots. Watch for pedestrians walking between vehicles, pets being walked, and children who may dart into driving lanes.

Sliding at low speeds can still cause serious injury. Extra caution in these shared spaces is essential.

Residential Streets

Residential streets may not receive the same level of snow removal or sanding as main roads. Ice can persist longer, especially in shaded areas. Children playing, people walking pets, and vehicles parked along the road increase the need for caution. Reduce speed and remain alert for sudden movement.

Winter driving safety applies everywhere—not just on major roads.

School Zones and Community Areas

School zones, playgrounds, and community facilities remain active throughout winter months. Snowbanks can limit visibility, and icy surfaces increase stopping distances.

Always obey reduced speed limits and be prepared for pedestrians crossing in unexpected locations. Winter conditions require extra patience in these areas.

Public Transit and Service Vehicles

Buses, snowplows, emergency vehicles, and delivery trucks operate frequently in winter conditions. These vehicles may stop suddenly, pull out unexpectedly, or require extra space to maneuver.

Give large vehicles additional room and avoid following too closely. Snowplows, in particular, may throw snow or create temporary whiteout conditions.

Final Thought on Community Driving

Winter driving is not just about protecting yourself—it is about protecting everyone around you. Reduced speeds, careful turns, and heightened awareness help create safer communities during challenging conditions.

Small adjustments in town and city driving can prevent serious injuries and collisions.

Winter parking lots present hidden hazards, including reduced traction, limited visibility, pedestrians, and pets.

Chapter 6

Medications, Health and Driver Readiness

Winter driving places additional physical and mental demands on drivers. Cold temperatures, reduced daylight, fatigue, and stress can all affect reaction time and judgment. Medications, health conditions, and overall readiness play a critical role in winter driving safety and should never be overlooked.

Being fit to drive is just as important as having a well-prepared vehicle.

How Medications Can Affect Driving

Many prescription and over-the-counter medications can impair driving ability, especially in winter conditions where reaction time and alertness are already challenged.

Medications that may affect driving include:

- Cold and flu remedies
- Allergy medications
- Pain medications
- Sleep aids
- Anti-anxiety or antidepressant medications

Side effects such as drowsiness, dizziness, slowed reaction time, or blurred vision can significantly increase risk when traction and visibility are reduced.

Always read medication labels carefully and consult a healthcare professional if you are unsure how a medication may affect your ability to drive.

Combining Medications and Cold Weather

Cold weather can intensify the effects of certain medications. Dehydration, fatigue, and prolonged exposure to cold may worsen side effects.

Never assume a medication that feels manageable in summer conditions will feel the same during winter driving. If you feel impaired or unwell, delay travel whenever possible.

Fatigue and Reduced Alertness

Winter driving often requires greater concentration. Darkness, glare from snow, and monotonous road conditions can increase fatigue.
Warning signs of fatigue include:

- Difficulty focusing
- Frequent yawning
- Drifting within lanes
- Slower reaction times

If you feel fatigued, take a break, switch drivers if possible, or postpone travel. Fatigue reduces your ability to respond safely to sudden winter hazards.

Vision and Winter Driving

Clear vision is essential during winter driving. Snowfall, blowing snow, glare, and low light conditions place additional strain on eyesight.

Ensure corrective lenses are current and appropriate. Keep spare glasses in your vehicle if needed, and wear sunglasses to reduce glare from snow during daylight hours.

If vision is compromised due to illness, fatigue, or medication, do not drive.

Chronic Health Conditions

Drivers with chronic health conditions should consider how winter conditions may affect their ability to drive safely. Cold temperatures and stress can worsen symptoms such as pain, stiffness, or reduced mobility.

Plan winter travel with additional time and flexibility. If symptoms worsen, avoid driving until conditions improve.

Sleep Apnea and Medical Devices

Drivers who rely on medical devices such as CPAP machines should plan carefully for winter travel. Power outages, extended delays, or overnight travel may affect device use.

Carry necessary supplies and ensure devices are functioning properly before long trips. If safe use cannot be ensured, consider delaying travel.

Emotional Readiness and Stress

Stress, anxiety, and emotional distraction can impair decision-making. Winter driving already requires heightened awareness, and emotional strain reduces the ability to respond calmly to changing conditions.

If you feel overwhelmed, rushed, or emotionally distracted, reassess the necessity of travel. Delaying a trip is often the safest choice.

Knowing When You Are Not Fit to Drive

One of the most important safety decisions is recognizing when you are not ready to drive. Health, medication effects, fatigue, or emotional stress can all compromise safety.

There is no obligation to drive when conditions or personal readiness are not appropriate. Making the decision to stay off the road protects you and others.

Final Reminder

Winter driving safety depends on more than road conditions and vehicle preparation. Your physical and mental readiness matters just as much.

Listen to your body, understand your medications, and choose safety over convenience.

Chapter 7

What to Do
if You Break Down

Breaking down in winter conditions can be stressful and dangerous, especially in cold temperatures or poor visibility. Knowing what to do—and what not to do—can significantly improve safety while waiting for assistance.

Most winter breakdowns are not immediately life-threatening, but improper responses can increase risk. Staying calm, visible, and prepared is key.

Stay With Your Vehicle When Possible

In most winter breakdown situations, it is safest to remain inside your vehicle. Your vehicle provides shelter from wind, cold, and passing traffic.

Leaving a vehicle in winter conditions can increase the risk of exposure, disorientation, or being struck by other vehicles. Unless help is clearly visible nearby, stay with your vehicle.

Make Your Vehicle Visible

Visibility is critical for safety and for being located by assistance.

Take the following steps:

- Turn on hazard lights
- Use reflective warning triangles or flares if safe to do so
- Keep headlights on when visibility is poor

If you must exit the vehicle, do so cautiously and remain aware of traffic.

Conserve Heat Safely

Run the engine periodically to generate heat, but ensure the exhaust pipe is clear of snow and ice. Blocked exhaust can allow carbon monoxide to build up inside the vehicle.

Crack a window slightly for ventilation if running the engine. Turn the engine off between heating cycles to conserve fuel.

Use blankets, extra clothing, and hand warmers to maintain body heat.

Call for Assistance Early

If you experience a breakdown, call for help as soon as possible. Contact:

- Roadside assistance services
- Local emergency services if you are in immediate danger
- A trusted contact if cell service is available

Do not wait until conditions worsen. Early communication improves response time.

Roadside Assistance Services

Memberships such as roadside assistance can be valuable, but response times may be delayed during winter storms or widespread incidents.

Understand the limitations of your service. Roadside assistance may not reach you immediately, especially in rural or severe weather conditions. Be prepared to wait safely.

If You Must Exit the Vehicle

Only exit your vehicle if it is absolutely necessary and safe to do so.

Wear high-visibility clothing if available, stay well away from traffic lanes, and avoid walking on icy surfaces. Never stand in front of or behind your vehicle where passing drivers may not see you.

Helping Others Safely

If you encounter another driver in distress, prioritize your own safety first. Park well off the roadway, activate hazard lights, and avoid placing yourself in traffic.

Call for assistance on their behalf if needed. Do not attempt risky maneuvers or roadside repairs in dangerous conditions.

Children and Passengers

Ensure passengers remain warm, calm, and inside the vehicle when possible. Use blankets and extra clothing to maintain warmth. Reassure children and keep them occupied to reduce stress during delays.

Final Guidance

Breaking down in winter is inconvenient, but panic and poor decisions can make it dangerous. Remaining with your vehicle, maintaining visibility, conserving heat, and calling for help early are the safest actions.

Preparation and calm decision-making can turn a winter breakdown into a manageable situation.

A disabled vehicle should be positioned safely off the roadway, with hazard lights on and warning triangles or road flares used when conditions allow.

Chapter 8

Roadside Assistance and Its Limits

Roadside assistance services can be an important safety resource during winter travel, but they are not a guarantee of immediate help.

Understanding what roadside assistance can—and cannot—provide is essential for realistic planning and safer decision-making.

Many drivers overestimate how quickly assistance will arrive during winter conditions. Storms, road closures, high demand, and limited access can all delay response times.

What Roadside Assistance Typically Provides

Most roadside assistance programs offer services such as:

- Battery boosting
- Flat tire assistance
- Lockout services
- Limited towing
- Fuel delivery

These services are useful for common winter issues, but they are subject to availability, weather conditions, and location.

Response Times in Winter Conditions

During winter storms or cold snaps, roadside assistance providers may receive a high volume of calls simultaneously. Response times can increase significantly, especially in rural areas or on secondary highways.

In some situations, assistance may be delayed for several hours. In extreme conditions, services may be temporarily suspended for safety reasons.

Drivers must be prepared to remain safely in their vehicle while waiting.

Location Matters

Your location plays a major role in response time and available services. Urban areas may offer faster response, but traffic congestion and weather can still cause delays. Rural and remote locations may have limited service coverage, fewer providers, and longer wait times.

Before travelling, understand whether your route passes through areas with limited roadside support.

Membership Limitations and Coverage

Roadside assistance memberships often have limitations, including:

- Maximum towing distance
- Restrictions on service frequency
- Exclusions for severe weather or off-road conditions

Review your membership details before winter travel. Do not assume all situations are covered.

When Roadside Assistance Is Not Enough

There are situations where roadside assistance alone may not be sufficient, including:

- Severe storms or whiteout conditions
- Highway closures
- Extreme cold
- Multiple vehicle incidents

In these cases, emergency services or highway authorities may need to coordinate response. Your priority should always be personal safety rather than immediate vehicle recovery.

Using Roadside Assistance Wisely

Call for assistance early when a problem arises. Provide accurate information about your location, vehicle condition, and surroundings.

Remain patient and follow instructions from service providers. Avoid attempting unsafe repairs or roadside maneuvers while waiting.

Preparing for Delays

Because roadside assistance may be delayed, winter preparedness remains essential even if you have coverage.

A winter emergency kit, warm clothing, and adequate fuel are critical backups when assistance is not immediately available.

Final Perspective

Roadside assistance is a valuable support, but it is not a substitute for preparation and sound judgment. Understanding its limitations helps drivers make safer choices during winter travel.

Planning for delays ensures you remain safe even when help takes time to arrive.

Chapter 9

Older Drivers

Winter driving can present additional challenges for older drivers, but age alone does not determine driving ability. Experience, preparation, and honest self-assessment play a greater role in safety than age itself.

Understanding how winter conditions interact with physical changes helps older drivers make informed, confident decisions.

Experience Is Valuable — Conditions Still Matter

Many older drivers have decades of experience and strong hazard-recognition skills. However, winter conditions reduce traction and visibility for everyone. Experience does not override the laws of physics.

Driving decisions should always be based on current conditions rather than past success. Respecting winter risks is a strength, not a limitation.

Reaction Time and Winter Conditions

Reaction time may change gradually with age, and winter driving demands faster responses to unexpected hazards such as skids, sudden stops, or reduced visibility.

Allowing additional following distance, reducing speed, and avoiding unnecessary trips during poor conditions help offset these challenges and improve safety.

Vision, Glare, and Low Light

Winter driving places extra strain on vision due to:

- Reduced daylight hours
- Glare from snow and ice
- Blowing snow and fog
- Low contrast environments

Ensure eye examinations are current and corrective lenses are appropriate. Keep windshields, mirrors, and headlights clean to maximize visibility.

If glare or reduced visibility becomes uncomfortable, avoid driving during those conditions.

Mobility and Physical Comfort

Cold temperatures can increase stiffness, joint pain, and reduced mobility. These factors may affect the ability to:

- Turn the head to check blind spots
- React quickly with steering or braking
- Exit the vehicle safely in an emergency

Plan winter travel with extra time and avoid rushing. Comfort and control are essential for safe driving.

Medications and Health Considerations

Older drivers are more likely to use medications that can affect alertness, coordination, or reaction time. Winter driving magnifies these effects due to increased cognitive demands.

Review medications regularly and avoid driving if side effects are present. If uncertain, consult a healthcare professional.

Choosing When and Where to Drive

Selective driving is a powerful safety tool. Many older drivers choose to:

- Avoid night driving in winter
- Limit travel during storms
- Stick to familiar routes
- Drive during daylight hours

These choices reduce risk without eliminating independence.

Planning Ahead for Safety

Before winter travel:

- Check weather and road conditions
- Ensure the vehicle is fully prepared
- Carry a winter emergency kit
- Let someone know your plans

Preparation provides peace of mind and reduces stress.

Family Conversations and Support

Open communication with family members supports safer winter driving decisions. These conversations should focus on safety and planning, not pressure or criticism.

Respectful dialogue helps maintain independence while prioritizing well-being.

Final Thought

Winter driving safety for older drivers is about awareness, preparation, and thoughtful decision-making. Experience combined with realistic self-assessment creates safer outcomes. Choosing caution over convenience protects both drivers and communities.

Chapter 10

Rural, Remote, and Long-Distance Travel

Winter travel in rural and remote areas presents unique challenges. Longer distances between communities, limited services, reduced cell coverage, and slower emergency response times increase risk when conditions deteriorate. Planning and preparation are essential when travelling beyond urban areas in winter.

Drivers should approach long-distance winter travel with caution, flexibility, and a willingness to change plans when conditions demand it.

Understanding Increased Risk

Rural highways and secondary roads may receive less frequent snow removal and maintenance than major routes. Ice, drifting snow, and reduced visibility can persist longer, particularly overnight or during storms.

Traffic volumes are often lower, which means fewer drivers to notice trouble or offer assistance. In these areas, self-sufficiency becomes critical.

Fuel, Distance, and Planning

Always begin rural or long-distance winter travel with a full tank of fuel. Unexpected delays, detours, or road closures can significantly extend travel time.

Plan routes carefully and identify fuel stops along the way. Avoid allowing fuel levels to drop too low, especially when services may be closed or inaccessible due to weather.

Communication and Coverage

Cell phone coverage can be unreliable or unavailable in remote areas. Do not assume you will be able to call for help at all times.
Carry:

- A fully charged phone
- A vehicle-compatible charging cable
- A backup battery pack
- A paper map in case GPS or digital navigation fails

Let someone know your route and expected arrival time before departure.

Weather Changes in Open Areas

Open terrain, such as prairies, mountain passes, and forested highways, is particularly vulnerable to rapid weather changes. Blowing snow, whiteout conditions, and strong winds can reduce visibility suddenly.

If conditions worsen:

- Reduce speed immediately
- Increase following distance
- Be prepared to stop or turn back

Do not assume conditions will improve further along the route.

Wildlife and Road Hazards

Wildlife encounters are more common in rural and remote areas. Reduced visibility and slippery roads increase the risk of collisions.

Scan roadsides continuously and reduce speed in areas known for wildlife activity. Avoid swerving suddenly, as loss of control may be more dangerous than impact.

Overnight Travel Considerations

Long-distance winter trips may require overnight stops. Weather conditions can change dramatically overnight, making morning travel unsafe.

Be prepared to adjust plans, extend stays, or delay departure if conditions deteriorate. Flexibility is a key component of winter travel safety.

Emergency Preparedness in Remote Areas

In remote locations, help may take hours to arrive. A comprehensive winter emergency kit is essential and should include:

- Extra warmth and clothing
- Food and water
- Emergency signaling devices
- Jumper cables or a battery booster
- Traction aids and basic tools

Preparation helps manage delays safely and reduces stress.

Knowing When to Turn Back

Turning back or stopping early is often the safest decision in remote winter travel. Pride or schedule pressure should never outweigh safety.

If visibility is poor, roads are impassable, or you feel uncertain, stop in a safe location or return to a known area with services.

Final Reminder

Rural, remote, and long-distance winter travel requires respect for distance, weather, and isolation. Preparation, communication, and flexibility are essential for safe outcomes.

The safest winter journey is one that adapts to conditions rather than pushing through them.

Keeping emergency contact information easily accessible helps first responders and reduces delays during winter incidents.

Appendix A
Emergency Information Pages

In an emergency, clear information can save time and reduce confusion. These pages are designed to be completed in advance and kept accessible inside your vehicle, such as in the glove compartment.

You may wish to print multiple copies of these pages for use in different vehicles or to share with family members. Emergency responders often look in the glove box for important information if a driver is unable to communicate.

We have included four sets of emergency pages so you can tear them out of the book (if you did the print version).

SECTION 1 — PERSONAL & VEHICLE INFORMATION

DRIVER INFORMATION	
Full Name	
Date of Birth	
Address	
Phone Number	

PRIMARY EMERGENCY CONTACT	
Full Name	
Relationship	
Contact Number	
Alternate Number	

SECONDARY EMERGENCY CONTACT	
Full Name	
Relationship	
Contact Number	
Alternate Number	

VEHICLE INFORMATION	
Vehicle Make & Model	
Vehicle Colour	
License Plate Number	
Insurance Provider	
Policy Number	

SECTION 2 — MEDICAL INFORMATION

DRIVER MEDICAL INFORMATION	
Medical Conditions	
Medications	
Allergies	
Medical Devices (e.g., CPAP, insulin)	
Physician or Clinic Name	
Physician Phone Number	

SECTION 3 — PET INFORMATION

ARE PETS TRAVELLING WITH YOU? YES ◯ NO ◯	
Type of Pet (s)	
Pet Name (s)	
Special Needs or Medications	
Veterinary Clinic Name	
Veterinary Clinic Phone	
Emergency Pet Contact	

SECTION 4 — ADDITIONAL NOTES

SECTION 1 — PERSONAL & VEHICLE INFORMATION

DRIVER INFORMATION	
Full Name	
Date of Birth	
Address	
Phone Number	

PRIMARY EMERGENCY CONTACT	
Full Name	
Relationship	
Contact Number	
Alternate Number	

SECONDARY EMERGENCY CONTACT	
Full Name	
Relationship	
Contact Number	
Alternate Number	

VEHICLE INFORMATION	
Vehicle Make & Model	
Vehicle Colour	
License Plate Number	
Insurance Provider	
Policy Number	

SECTION 2 — MEDICAL INFORMATION

DRIVER MEDICAL INFORMATION	
Medical Conditions	
Medications	
Allergies	
Medical Devices (e.g., CPAP, insulin)	
Physician or Clinic Name	
Physician Phone Number	

SECTION 3 — PET INFORMATION

ARE PETS TRAVELLING WITH YOU? YES ○ NO ○	
Type of Pet (s)	
Pet Name (s)	
Special Needs or Medications	
Veterinary Clinic Name	
Veterinary Clinic Phone	
Emergency Pet Contact	

SECTION 4 — ADDITIONAL NOTES

SECTION 1 — PERSONAL & VEHICLE INFORMATION

DRIVER INFORMATION	
Full Name	
Date of Birth	
Address	
Phone Number	

PRIMARY EMERGENCY CONTACT	
Full Name	
Relationship	
Contact Number	
Alternate Number	

SECONDARY EMERGENCY CONTACT	
Full Name	
Relationship	
Contact Number	
Alternate Number	

VEHICLE INFORMATION	
Vehicle Make & Model	
Vehicle Colour	
License Plate Number	
Insurance Provider	
Policy Number	

SECTION 2 — MEDICAL INFORMATION

DRIVER MEDICAL INFORMATION	
Medical Conditions	
Medications	
Allergies	
Medical Devices (e.g., CPAP, insulin)	
Physician or Clinic Name	
Physician Phone Number	

SECTION 3 — PET INFORMATION

ARE PETS TRAVELLING WITH YOU? YES ⬤ NO ⬤	
Type of Pet (s)	
Pet Name (s)	
Special Needs or Medications	
Veterinary Clinic Name	
Veterinary Clinic Phone	
Emergency Pet Contact	

SECTION 4 — ADDITIONAL NOTES

SECTION 1 — PERSONAL & VEHICLE INFORMATION

DRIVER INFORMATION	
Full Name	
Date of Birth	
Address	
Phone Number	

PRIMARY EMERGENCY CONTACT	
Full Name	
Relationship	
Contact Number	
Alternate Number	

SECONDARY EMERGENCY CONTACT	
Full Name	
Relationship	
Contact Number	
Alternate Number	

VEHICLE INFORMATION	
Vehicle Make & Model	
Vehicle Colour	
License Plate Number	
Insurance Provider	
Policy Number	

SECTION 2 — MEDICAL INFORMATION

DRIVER MEDICAL INFORMATION	
Medical Conditions	
Medications	
Allergies	
Medical Devices (e.g., CPAP, insulin)	
Physician or Clinic Name	
Physician Phone Number	

SECTION 3 — PET INFORMATION

ARE PETS TRAVELLING WITH YOU? YES ⚪ NO ⚪	
Type of Pet (s)	
Pet Name (s)	
Special Needs or Medications	
Veterinary Clinic Name	
Veterinary Clinic Phone	
Emergency Pet Contact	

SECTION 4 — ADDITIONAL NOTES

Provincial Resources and Road Information

Road conditions and weather can change rapidly during winter travel. Checking official provincial resources before and during a trip provides critical information about closures, hazards, and travel advisories.

The following list includes official road information websites, roadside assistance organizations, and emergency contact guidance for each province. Website addresses may change over time; if a link is unavailable, search using the organization name.

PROVINCE-BY-PROVINCE RESOURCES

British Columbia

Road Conditions & Webcams:
DriveBC.ca

Roadside Assistance:
BCAA (British Columbia Automobile Association)

Emergency Services: 911
(Police, Fire, Ambulance)

Alberta

Road Conditions & Webcams:
511.alberta.ca

Roadside Assistance:
AMA (Alberta Motor Association)

Emergency Services: 911
(Police, Fire, Ambulance)

Saskatchewan

Road Conditions:
Highways.gov.sk.ca

Roadside Assistance:
CAA Saskatchewan

Emergency Services: 911
(Police, Fire, Ambulance)

Manitoba

Road Conditions & Cameras:
Manitoba511.ca

Roadside Assistance:
CAA Manitoba

Emergency Services: 911
(Police, Fire, Ambulance)

Ontario

Road Conditions & Traffic
Cameras:
Ontario.ca/511

Roadside Assistance:
CAA Ontario

Emergency Services: 911
(Police, Fire, Ambulance)

Quebec

Road Conditions & Traffic
Cameras:
Quebec511.info

Roadside Assistance:
CAA-Québec

Emergency Services: 911
(Police, Fire, Ambulance)

New Brunswick

Road Conditions:
Gnb.ca
Roadside Assistance:
CAA Atlantic
Emergency Services: 911
(Police, Fire, Ambulance)

Nova Scotia

Road Conditions:
511.novascotia.ca
Roadside Assistance:
CAA Atlantic
Emergency Services: 911
(Police, Fire, Ambulance)

PEI

Road Conditions:
PrinceEdwardIsland.ca
Roadside Assistance:
CAA Atlantic
Emergency Services: 911
(Police, Fire, Ambulance)

Newfoundland

Road Conditions:
NL511.ca
Roadside Assistance:
CAA Atlantic
Emergency Services: 911
(Police, Fire, Ambulance)

Before Winter Travel Checklist:

☐ Check weather forecast
☐ Check road conditions and webcams
☐ Confirm roadside assistance coverage
☐ Fuel vehicle
☐ Inform someone of your route and arrival time
☐ Carry a winter emergency kit

www.ingramcontent.com/pod-product-compliance
Lightning Source LLC
Chambersburg PA
CBHW081547040426

42448CB00015B/3245